MW00876049

August @2023

Mark Borisyuk. Geller

The power of Love~

The knower and known of life are love, Love is in and for itself. Love is greater than the sum of all our knowledge. Love is the projection of death thus, love is immortal. The spirit sees life as growth, or flowering. In love, we feel that what we do not know, the penny of the sun in his soul, each sun to love by the heart, and to then aspire be with a knowing outlet, that love, is the tattoo of God.

Guess ~

A Barny (Troubled) lover make up of one part, a beat of life and a love the heart, the stars are them pebbles, apple smiles no isles, color of her brown eyes, and tweeted or charm of her old heaven in thine sweet tender, kissed lips where her temple is mystery much like lemon, in tea, I love you all the more, lovely lady queen, morning sun and then be an evening gown, purple roses, and cherry cheeks, around be my lips to her heart into be tulips, tender lemon, on a lemon I can on her eyes, the eyes cup beside her temple, as my tips at her smile, A down your cherry of cup on a charm, and bee as in the babe to sweet lover surrender the apple cup, and in a pho, a nose to my your sweet cherish, in like much love much sweet open to watch heaven, the loved mind a raspberry finger be at my finger, put this heart on an apple mystery goes, is love like an lemon insane kisses a sweet lipstick, a nose to breathe open her sweet cherry hips, her apples art smiles at the heart every eve rest and thine, dime pecan eyes, I kissed.

Binder Tree~

Breakfast In the old day,
one bosom round, little
past summer, brail river
and valley, half point that
would quiet, but enough
taught as their medium
horse, small fate uniform,
days like a mule, be a RIP
Ruske harp, as heavy the
pumpkin, all women said
one love, but we cannot
vouch all in us, in winkles,
the thoughts, words say, I
am, vitamin D.

Jewish Prose~

I am a blessed knight with
my wings to see and feel.
The angel shall make a
vow for you. Thus, you will
praise and rise to love as
kindly that grace can be
dove(n) since birth is a
vine hath, for all mankind,
the fruit for all mankind
made to each divine a
voice.

Cigarette~

The sky the purple rose,
no doubt she bare cherry
cheeks, around the heart
for her tulips, these be
their wakeful mind, and
weather leaves summer,
the sun recedes in song,
she sparks my love with
singing, their warmth of
curls for sun orchards, the
breadth of life to be the
morn, the splinters in her
beauty, oh gosh how love

8

is dumb, we're mead the entity within a sweetness to honey, the harsh wind will come, but reality, ask the immortal hawk, his will is to fly and sweep the honey's tooth, so ripe and fare are apple doodle in palette, O' cherry teat.

Boom@

Hero art child, each field recouple wheels, letter price – touching bye, The leaves the dole in prate, jungle drain trees fall as, knot, knot sickness and diamond sock, about evil nothing bad hat, brain survival be to serve dog, hi dear Jerry queue in Braxton Dr. weep a snip for balloon, I am a hero, but were couldn't, count pioneer in yellow, cleave chaser wonder mirrored, class the heavy pump in kin, kipper jean and swim bean, tux bear lollypop for our wind, we created the water lime, been under the spray from weather tooth rear end the cool pea, in tree, face the wall in gang the boat heart, I do not know a word ferry, most of all I care to pay toll, a wash my path with under, I want the call to blame all, my brother gone in wheat...

under the poster I am
short, and under the gun
be as awe I am in, Russian
roulette in sum rum, can
love not see chicken run,
let us begin…

ROSE

Love is a rose in the sky

In a dim, moon light night

A flight and hummingbird

O' cherry tree

A spark ignites a Jewel of fire. A firefly and distand stars. Love is a stairway of heaven. A nile of endless Sun. A beating of a rose for faith is molded touch, The petals turn to march a hart. To the moon love

turns a sword. Like a rose
that turns to be sun.

The Hand~

The blessing of ours love is
good in part free from
each a heart to each for
hand, to each judgement
and to each hand is the
dance in sand, their beat
for the world is peaceful
for an sole feel in part of

each pebble from a heart
become endless blossom
hart being as understood,
an wood attached in well,
and feeling good miracle.

The Sun~

How beautiful the sun,

To thought

To thought

To thought...

The Bee~

You have wounded the bee. The bee cheated on you. Who carried you the aspirin. Bee the wounded bee.

Otter~

Sun asp to touch,

Odder pea pay's

Love is Artistical,

Also tooth fears,

Le tuna disfruta.

Galina ~

As passion turn tears feel
a flower in heart, evening
just hurts to love as penny
grey, again at night be
then a loving hart as
husked, jest the breath
take kissed and love at
pave, tore and pure take
best my lovely sun as dart,
on my flume I then invite a

peach or sourest grape
however roses read purest
my love into be my kissed
be from my abode heart,
by the star part, all dark
parts in the light, but
chase of pleasure finance,
succored opuses, diaries,
too piety, and media rock.

My Lady America~

You are the moon across
my heart,

The stars are the pebbles
in our hands,

Place a pebble of my
heart, in the sea,

The sea shall swallow our
love again,

We shall sail the red string
of the sun,

In my coldest of nights, I
cried,

To be a fire to the stars
that you see.

The Red String~

Love is being blindfolded by the eyes and felt in the heart. If love is to be as then a whore between the sheets, then I am the lines in between the truth and our love. Because love cannot to be but as dark mystery, then it is a prank on the surface. with the letters being The Red String.

21

Heart to Heart~

Love is always from the hart as your start, a galaxy open as being an dreamt, messages fall in your carry and dutiful speak in worth, Waterbed and Crystal a child pray, and moved to Eve the neighbor, which at one time the deed in an play, angelic children then speaking to another smile, in their tender heart going, there had eardrum willingly been, to bye and bye and bye, and find it and find it...

Prose~

sentiment that the dipper comes out at two in the morning is not too mine. Amusement am I cannot be sentimental. Although, I am two in different reasons of with thought, which at once scientifically is proven must but be and observationally and thereof a deductively, although inductively: could be generalized and poetic inclined, okay! so there are four, in one hour resting or sleeping with REM, asleep cycles. To the fourth width a REM computed each cycle between the forty and the so as five minutes: so, five times then a four is twenty suggesting dividing by ten to as equaling the two. And tangent there we hold the driving wheel be to at ten and at two. However, in a twenty-four with evening or morning cycle mine being cosign from two and from forty, been added at twenty. And as I cosign exists per

24

orbital circle around the two spooks in the morning hour from dipper one and, from dipper two. There are two time zones split in forty and eight minutes.

Thus, Psychology deduced suggesting that ad a cosign force forty and five minutes equaling to having to being subtracted was additional 8 minutes + or - REM 4 cycles.

Ad Do Sunset~

Thus, my heart is a seal or bond, to be with you in our love is to give this an oath, from letters which as sign be cry, an engineer cannot blame, under a fortnight to a farce, as this breast the pleasure sees, the desert flower, distance, a morning the mistress be as honest, come in the silenced mind,

I'd golden sun in the apple bye, leaves are dropping, I cannot then know how or

why! as light flowing bye,
sailing wonder, better their
dunes of sand, shared, to
hopefully again, and loved,
passed a warm-warm, tear
and which that I can have
in the tomorrow dear.

Made in the USA
Columbia, SC
22 August 2023